Torment Of The Poetic Spirit

Elaine Sadie Lerato Madisa

Pharos Books

ISBN: 978-93-91103-93-4
eISBN: 978-93-91103-95-8

Publisher: **Pharos Books (P) Ltd.**
Plot No.-55, Main Mother Dairy Road
Pandav Nagar, East Delhi-110092
Phone: +14049995474
WhatsApp: +14049995474
E-mail: sales@pharosbooks.in
Website: www.pharosbooks.in
Edition: 2021

Torment of the Poetic Spirit
Elaine Sadie Lerato Madisa

Contents

Introduction

They would ask why poetry—and in response— why not, the art that's brutal truth with ink and paper. It has power to heal, break or build I chose to motivate, heal and inspire.

Bare in mind it's not just a gift but a calling. Here lies the bones spirit quickened to life and now existing as flesh. A book of poems that draw canvas of the sad, joyful, nerve wrecking times of a poet's life. My gift to you poetry and spoken word.

Acknowledgments

First and foremost I thank God for the gift to speak and write poetry realizing it's his mandate manifesting and me being the mouthpiece. I thank my family and friends for supporting my art. To my publisher and manager I am forever indebted to you.

My church True Light Ministries and Glorious Cloud arts group for providing me platform and support. All have poured diesel to my gift, I am grateful. Mum, thank you for giving me life and bountiful support for my venture.

Pour Diesel To My Flame

I met a guy I think he loves like Jesus
His strength reminds me of Samson
And simplicity yet anointed like David
His Dependency reminds me of Job on God
Welcoming like Boaz with Ruth
does he really fit the prescription
or it's just an illusion

I have never been good with writing love poems
Exciting fantasy, romance to call
to attention the crowd
So then I decide to write upon the scroll
One day who stands worthy will be able to unfold
Dear Jesus please let God get this memo
I send this as burning incense of sweet aroma
So then I decided as Jesus is groom
I will write to him

My role was never to be cupid aim with an arrow
But be bride in cleansing
I am in a season of preparation
Why be risk takers if he placed bridge
over the red sea
That I cross over in chariots of liberty
Now let me just download and unravel
the love flame that had gone off

Before I was like a scent of a dead animal
None wanted to associate or acquaint to
If the gas trucks hit and threw me by the roadside
I wasn't even qualifying for a pick-up truck
Couldn't blot out being blameless without spot
No.. no.. no..
I was a third degree kind of criminal
I'm the reincarnated, born again, disappeared spots

Now look at how the flame came about
Passed through fire but did not scorch me
Almost drank two, three cups drowning
Somehow I made it stayed afloat
Stood before your eyes trembling with fear that what
if the first word that came out would
sound completely ridiculous
You might want to stand and take your leave
I'm the reincarnated, born again and so are you

So now I gave you reason to listen
Mission to hear
His love seeks no wrong, fault or wrong turn
Thank him for the dark for you bear
Testimony of the light
Thank him for the test for you preached testimony
Aim for the moon who knows
we might land among stars
Most important don't lose direction
of your flame keep it burning
Dear Jesus please I beg make sure
God gets this memo
While you at it
Pour diesel to my flame

Behind The Smile

Behind the smile
The clouds gathered as soldier's formation
War for precipitation to embrace
With tears of why me
I didn't hear David's soothing harp
But anger and rage lighting to my ears
The sun did not shine bright like a diamond
Neither the light on the hill top glaze the universe
I was shunned by hells darkness accompanied
By an army of betrayal of angel Michaels troop
How many more sleepless night
Because atleast you share the memo
So I may pack a tissue, a glass of water to replace
the river Jordan I am opening to flow
Tears have lately become my bestie
I wonder does this mourning season take long
Because honey I am hoping for my new dawn

Reintroduce

Let me re Introduce myself
This is a new crowd and new season
Maybe for a minute I lost my cool and calm
Lost my aim and my lane
Ran out of pace to race
Regardless of my misfortune
This time around Ent rouge necessary
I remember he said I will stand among kings
Let me clarify this he did not say
you will stand as a servant among them
Rather wine and dine
And briefing about his gracious mercy
Because last time I checked he never runs out
Not out of mercy, grace love or favor
Not power to perform
Or strength to strategize among the vitals of success
I mean he enables its existence
His creator of possibilities
Doesn't leave nor forsake
Let me re introduce you
You a royal kind of brand
Engraved his word circumference of your heart
Likeness of the unparalleled and unbeatable God
Should I go on least your doubts scale him
on a one to zero

When he rose in human flesh as the only go to hero
Wait a minute did I just prick where it matters
Have my words silenced your anxiety
that was left untamed
Anxious for the prophetic
but not the petitions of prayer
Supplication was freely given
Application was freely given
You needed to act upon the declarations
But somehow you want to drive opposite direction on a one way road
Is this how you breed accidents uncalled for
During daylight when the sun stands a pillar of light
Winter sky cleared by existence of the blue sky
That they lied and said it's your limit
But last I checked only his perfect fitted plan
Describes your outmost potential
He said he gave dominion and authority
But even that you take for granted

What If/Midnight Poetic

What if the same world that took first place
To mock, ridicule and question
my obligiance to the encrypted law
Now turns to ask how do you do it
What if sleeping beauty did not just gain a prince?
She gained a king seated on the throne
No need to impress me with a mustang
As if the price he set forth wasn't enough
Because the only love he ever had
Was hanging knocked and nailed to a cross
Mere wood not worthy to pitch a bonfire
Last time I checked he died worthy
last the lady broke to his feet
the last drip of her alabaster...
Or the only garment love had. .power was ripped by the need of weeping soul in distress
I mean Cornelius gave but didn't run out
Job had it but it was all taken all the love
But guess what remained the true love
Same that allowed for the devil to rip him off
As if procession wasn't enough disability
His health my God deterioration at its best
I mean is this a man of test and trials
or a spirit at war and rage
What you want from us were good deeds not enough

count as remembrance of me
You placed me in a world of glitz and glamour
But guess what you got served
Because I am not even searching
for the fame and fortunes
My spirit, soul and countenance is content with the
wisdom that comes by your word
The wealth of owning pieces of art
And a chance for them to realize
it's the Grace she operates in
Because scientific knowledge alone
doesn't fit the criteria
Don't blame the professors for what mere human
explanation could not define...
because its divine
Hhhmmm I laughed, listen
Not to the train tracks alarming or the music in your
room soothing your ears
What if you could listen closely?
To his voice that second guesses
Your doubtful actions that have always
and I mean always let him down...
Then you have nerve to say why
didn't he give me a sign
I mean he spoke in rebuke and command
But still your stubbornness didn't bother to bow

Pandemic Struck

It struck front doors to birthday celebrations
Resolutions of year 2020
Dreams, ambitions disrupted
One case of previous year in a foreign land
To the universe at large catastrophe had fallen
Now the anxiety about our tomorrow building up To the home-less where would the next meal
be coming from
For upon busy streets was a penny worth while
of a shopaholic
Trolley of groceries, party accessories

A stare in the frontline has the she officers
Giving their last breathe for the sake of a nation
Accustomed to social distance, mask on
We live a life of adherence to sanitizers
As if it was not enough
Every motor vehicle drivers
In listing names of the infected and affected
The ones who escaped or might
Just be an invasion of contact tracing
After a blissful yet fearful stay at home
Education awaits cautious teachers
The economy has faced drastic times
Private companies seeking finance to stay afloat

Hijacking every hesitating client
to place their purchase
To our fighters ministers of decisions
That could dictate survival from death sentences
Or bring the world to entire catastrophe
Our trust are in prayers and incense sent to heavens
Petitioning God to have mercy
Least we killed by a devil
we can't see with naked eyes
But behold its brutality in the physical creations
With us included to the equation
Food and clothing shops have ascribed new culture
The feared way of life is our new normal

Nurses, doctors and scientists in search of
New heaven of cure and suppressing biotics
To clear what now is but was once not
Suspicions have led to lab tests gone wrong
Does our fate lie in hands of economies awaiting to
finance their luxury with medications of
uncertainty?
Or mere individual who would love to save every bit
of life the universe carries.

Palm Of Initiative

I speak to young minds engulfed within
Borders of a garage system belittled ideas
Never amounted to a penny
But to their dismay stands to make millions
Associated with knowledge of slumber
You rose to the occasion
And your light finally brought forth silver lining
I wore this skirt today to remind them
African hands where manipulating threads of colour Initiating style and sophistication
I'm humbled by the street vendor
In the scorching sun
She let patience tag along
Even though she goes home
having sold couple of hotdogs
Lined up selling one product
unto satisfaction of consumers
Shall we take it out of the streets?
To shaky built markets
To the butcher who befriended a sharp pointed blade
Slicing upon fresh oxen thigh

I wasn't born legend but somehow
Living under shadows of my fellow siblings
beyond average

I tried to ascribe unto
the worlds prescription of success
Which was written with overdose
of determination to persevere

Again I speak unto you
Placing your skill and talent
on bedrock level of the soil
Who told you to tame your wildest dreams?
Explore and remember I mentor
You to rise above the limiting factors
Business lies on the palm of your hands
Not some foreign approval for you to begin
The miracle is built right from the inside
Now wise up and build the initiative
I assure you youth, adult you hold key
to this economy

Essence Of Love

We been tied by love in holy matrimony
Today we exist as one flesh in his likeness
Belongings we share with hope of
Entrusting teamwork, compliments of cooperation
With aroma of worship reigning in our house
We been marked as his called ones
We not perfect but we made with perfection
We then take each day to ascribe unto the dosage of
our creation to satisfy his perfection...
We not Romeo or Juliet
Or any existing Shakespeare tale
But we genuine you and I (put names of the couple)
We exist to write a new tale,
fulfil our own design of a fairytale

I vow with your crazy habits
my words won't change
But through his character tolerate and accept
Placing you in his hands
as one I have faith to exist side by side with
That one day our off springs will take after
But still in amaze you will ask
Who do you take after,
Look who's talking
The original who begot the photocopy

Have you looked in the mirror lately?
I didn't know I would have in common
with a stranger
From a foreign land we spoke multitude languages
But we shared one of love in common the most
One of creativity, sophistication yet
It was simple and elegance at play

Crown Of Grace

Curbed up in a mother's womb placenta habitat
infiltrating agents of growth
To and from tussled winds of change
On my back I carried you child that tomorrow
you rise to mine diamonds of divinity
Portraying truth and soul
As we put hands together applauding
We celebrate uniqueness, boldness, courage
You have portrayed when the gravity
pushed you down your rocket of perseverance
pushed you to greater heights
Standing on two feet carrying nations,
Nurturing for success
Twist and turn as you rinse off the dust of
discouragement that had attached
To the six inch stiletto
And hem of garment of Grace
That you wear graceful as a swan
Red as scarlet
White as snow
As the industry enabled your existence now able
to rise in male dominated industries
Remember the beads incorporated with love
You sold to adorn yet another lady...
Rainbow skirt sewn to each thread
Precisely class and elegance

They threw me to the ground but I came back to the
Altitude with strength unbreakable
My spirit rose from torment, my soul shouted Hope,
Love, Faith, and Self-belief
Like Hannah I prayed for heaven treasures
encrypted in my name they call me drunk
But it was the zeal that was burning ablaze

They say a journey of a thousand steps begins with
one step now we take the first
Maya Angelou I rise a woman of substance

The Battle

You said we wrestle not against flesh and blood
But principalities, strongholds, spiritual wickedness,
but somehow
Felt defeated when the enemy ventured
to disarmer my amour
I could not preach put on the whole amour of Christ
neither the iron nor bronze seemed
to shut off arrows directed to my arena
Your word they said is a sword somehow in battle
I misplaced tell me
Is it really shaper than any double edged sword
Or the definition sounded fascinating
Compared to fiction of Percy Jackson lighting thief
Or Hercules, can Hobbs and Shaw define?
Are you still listening God?

Because I remember wishing for a sign
And all I got were ashes of burnt paper
Of poems that never made it to eyes of the beholder
Apart from the author spiraling of emotions
I put those in the fire..
wishing it would not scotch me
But somehow the boiling oil and steam of iron
burned surface of my skin marks
standing as affirmation

Affirmation...???
You reminded me be still fearless, quiet
As I behold you salvation
I failed because firstly like the wavering, tossing
and turning waves of the sea
I could not see when you put a doorway of victory
I mean actually had to get harder
before it went softer
I quit on the edge of a miracle
For I scratched surface and became
afraid to ruin my medicure

I lost steadiness of my feet to be delivered
I let deceit of the evil one trip me falling into a pit
That really was for his fall not mine
What about the angels you sent into my life
I was still fighting to understand their humanity
And failed to see you uncover their heavenly
Focused more on the pain
temporary passerby created
Failed to see the shoulder of the
angel there to comfort me
The one whom you created to be for life eternal
Failed to see the joy pressed down my direction,
by glittery of my eyes from tears

Poetry Is My Drug

I'm a, Poetaholic…
Don't blame me blame the dosage
of inspiration they feed me
In attempt to a maybe I will turn down a few stages
and shy away from an open mic
I feel as high as cloud nine is supposedly

I'm labeled insane I agree I mean what normal mind
is defeated by joy of Shakespeare lines
Still though I'm sane if my vocabulary seems to
make sense to planed rhyme and somehow excite
rhythm of the crowd
And keep the cheering on their feet
Convince the nods of a few heads
I think I make sense, that should count
as approval for the complete
Idiocy coming out from my mouth

The volume of pain my heart
chooses to speak through ink
Word of mouth was too painful
Instead I taught heart to grow numb
That way would be like hitting a rock
with a stick with no emotions it won't feel

But with time as one hit by Moses water comes out
maybe too much pressure you have enforced
Have you forgotten it's an organ it grows weary
Why overburden it with such hot to handle
What about the deceit
Did it feel right to lure me in
and cuddle me with lies
Rather than confront me head on with the truth
That would break me but one day build me up again
Lesson prolonged not decades of fake living

It's my dosage of hallucinogens somehow
when I take it I see myself in another world
of only possibilities, abilities
Floating on top of living waters said
to flow out of the heart diligently try to keep
Somehow it was torn between two worlds of do you
have faith yet you lost hope
Crumbled vision when I didn't write it down
Forgotten dream forgot how to live it, when I saw it
It's the only thing that makes sense when
All seems to fail
The soothing pill to the pain
Portion of subscription allow me to settle
Escaped edge of depression

Somehow despites all odds you gave me purpose
Ultimate reason to why I want to wake up
Poetry is my pleasant drug

You Called Me Beautiful

You called me, beautiful today
Even though my eyebrows were not
on fleek and face spotlessly clean
Even though my hair was not looking
up to date with the weather or season
Hello bank account never checked in
You called me Beautiful even though
you saw deep within my imperfections
my wrongs were overflowing a cup of gold or silver
Still you chose to call me beautiful

Free And Liberated

Don't know if you understand your freedom
You see he was sentenced guilty
Even though you were caught red handed
blood dripping
From your hands of guilt
Charged for sin not even his hands
Worthy to commit
Nailed to a cross put in to shame
His crown of Grace
Just For you

Nelson Mandela said it's a long walk to freedom
In agreement I said
I was given the word to release me from
Chains and cages breaking my shackles
Setting free from being carcass for vultures
To prey upon
Like Maya Angelou I rise
But it isn't about the rise
But how well do I get back up
when pushed and provoked right to the ground
I am a cage and chain breaker a shackle demolisher
I am free and liberated

Janetiks said I will wait
For one who loves unconditionally like Jesus

To deserve my heart
Not one to whisper empty sweet nothings
And be guard against cupid's arrow
Not Mr right now
Mr right my knight in shining amour
I am just a call fairytale into reality
Maybe in my long awaiting I will be groomed
To attain title of proverbs 31 female
But I had to go on journey of self-discovery
While searching God find me
Place Jesus as my chief corner stone
Fight to surmount to his Grace
And rest in his embrace
I am a chains breaker shackle slayer
I am free and liberated

I am the same girl u come across in school corridors
Seats in third row and hesitates to raise hand in class
I'm not noticed and only seen
by those who choose to
To you I'm invisible to God
I'm a famous legend on the rise
Not meaning to boast but show
that's how much God values
and regards me and you
I have broken my chains
I'm free and liberated

Some say she quiet and reserved
But like an atomic bomb I'm building up countdown
Give me time and mic so I explode
Not with my speech
But words of the potter who molded me

Thee undefined creation
Of the unparalleled messiah
I have broken my chains I'm free and liberated

Yes I'm not your perfect poet preacher or praiser
But still he finds way to see beyond my
Countless flaws
I have tried to ignore how embarrassed I feel
When you gaze to my face in search for beauty
I myself fighting to discover
But they say our scars are definition of our beauty
I have broken my chains I am free and liberated

Peculiar, patient like Mother Theresa
Not pertaining to patterns of this universe
You cut from a royal garment of grace
Meant to be outstanding, extraordinary
Your slit does not match one of the latest altezza
but very much of beauty
I'm a cage breaker..
I'm set free freedom candidate liberated soul

Minor Setbacks For Major Comeback

Laid upon the tomb that spit him
 could not contain him
A comeback of three defined days
Brewing a glow far beyond
purchase of dollar and naira
I have been digged deep six feet
But yet I seem to have risen six times
two times higher above pure
Sea level does not dictate the height of my flight

My scars have run deep could not fade
Bruises too shallow could not perish
But yet defined simplicity and beauty
Curved upon my face his likeness
I'm unlike the ordinary
The Anointed Human being
Like a vessel of Gold I carry honour
in hands of the Potter

Fury furnace could not contain me
River Jordan spit me out by the riverside
Maybe my taste was bitter to swallow
Circumstance fought like Goliath
But faith as little as a masters seed
Dropped it down with a stone
They engraved failure for my walk

But jumping above the pit dug for me
I settled in the table of my enemies
Looked them straight up in the eye
I have intimidated many with my success
To their dismay
I assure more is yet to come

Dont blame it on me
He named me.Legend before my existence
Adorned me with love
I give away so much
Not hoping to gain anything in return
But more of him as I empty alot of me
Let him smoothen my impeferctions and raw edges
I have qualified for this run
Keep your lane as I do justice to mine
Behold world you shall be like a footstool
When he raises the warrior of valour in me

Hungry for his word thirsty for his Wisdom
Fill Oh God with a quench of Righteousness
Will I qualify as Saints will be marching in
A year of all come back
Everything the devil stole shall report itself missing
No need for police statements
GOD fights theft better
I speak to nations as his mouthpiece
For I cannot be held accountable
for his work at hand
Do not crucify the messenger
Accept first the message at hand
Young one awaken from your zone of slumber

Show evidence with your harvest
Truly the laborers are few
Pray to the master sets you among the counted
Has your faith and works accounted
Your name to reappear in book of remembrance

A year I'm dusting my failure
Open hands success is near
A door away let me meet it upon the balcony
Tears of agony have paid visit
But now allow me to be selfish with my joy
I have been counted as blessed let me rejoice
I don't know what tomorrow brings
But I know God has me in this one
It's not over until
He sends chariots to my rescue
I'm coming back greater
don't miss me in my absence

Ignite Me With Force Of A Dynamite

Ignite me with force of a dynamite
Unlike Peter three times I will not deny
With utterance of my tongue teach me Hannah
to pray till dawn breaks
Yes I might not be given Samuel but treasures
Of heaven neatly wrapped in insufficient Grace
Not chasing miracles or prophecies
For your word in it I found words, phrases, rhythm,
rhyme all possible
Fame and fortune of the world
mean nothing, zero
If my name does not reappear each day upon the
book of life in day of remembrance
Upon the red carpet served on a silver platter
For in the beginning created in the image of God
Thousand times like Ruth upon Naomi
Only I disrespected I had shades of loyalty
Wanted to know if this thing would benefit me
Yes you right I was selfish
Wait a minute I am selfish with his love and words
would rather curve in my heart
Allowing him to have all of me
None of the pieces for man to explore and devour
Can I get an Amen for I am taken
Not with a ring or date night

Assuming within chaff extracted
by the winnowing wind
Ignite me with strength of Samson
Not allowing sinuses sent by Delilah
To block, this is the air that I breathe
Breathe life oh God Ntokozo Mbambo got me right
Like clay manipulate with your finger tips
my rough edges, crooked shape
Least they focus on my imperfections
I am not fit to wear the crown
Called among saints to be marching in Ignite me if only I am
worthy like Jesus ready to die for a sinner like me
Not assumptions but assurance I am not forgotten
God knows my name
Ignite me if only I am worthy

Awake Lioness

A woman a mother a daughter
Graceful as a swan like the lion of Judah
Speaks and wants to be heard
Like Ruth stays obedient to her in laws

Firm in worship like Ntokozo Mbambo
An inspiration to multitudes like Nelson Mandela
Leader of charisma like Barack Obama
Of poetic intelligence like Maya Angelou
Universe stands amazed at her beauty and gaze
Urge to love unconditionally
And hope selflessly
And speak blamelessly she is a woman
The Awake Lioness
Her sophistication brightens her inner glow
Like a flower her colour awakens her blossom
And stand out from the rest
Her presence is completeness of the crowd
For not only does she keep intact
she builds and nurtures

Her pride like the silk fabric that
Slithers and hugs upon her body
Her high stilettos
That leaves a remark as makes way into a room
She is a woman
The Awake Lioness

Tormented By A Poetic Spirit

I am tormented by a poetic spirit
It gives me no time out like epilepsy
Now and then I encounter a seizure
Biology could not comprehend this one
Scientists leave me to die
For they fail at hundredth attempt
To try explain my infirmity

Nurse this is messing with my head
Lobatse hospital would not cut out for me
Leave me by the door of retards
Maybe I will find my way to the nerds
And crack open their heads
And find cure to torment of my poetic

Oh God take it away
No bring it back it completes me
Bishop do not deliver me
I believe it's doing something great on the inside
Prophet I believe prophesy won't do me justice
Take a seat behind the Bishop
This one is another dimension
Of the prophetic manifested
Leave me to my poetic spirit

I have made it my heart is racing like bolt
I try grab door handle to the courtroom
And guess who is judge, it's God
And Jesus the Advocate
Do we really need to go for trial?
I have already won this battle

As I ponder upon my mistakes
Trying to rewrite my retakes
Gaze upon the sky a cloud so far off
But now the rain has come
Let it pour down on me
As I embrace the torment of my poetic spirit